THIS BOOK BELONGS TO

_____

START DATE

_____

SHE READS TRUTH

EXECUTIVE

FOUNDER/CHIEF EXECUTIVE OFFICER
Raechel Myers

CO-FOUNDER/CHIEF CONTENT OFFICER
Amanda Bible Williams

CHIEF OPERATING OFFICER/
CREATIVE DIRECTOR
Ryan Myers

EXECUTIVE ASSISTANT
Catherine Cromer

EDITORIAL

CONTENT DIRECTOR
John Greco, MDiv

MANAGING EDITOR
Jessica Lamb

PRODUCT MANAGER, KIDS READ TRUTH
Melanie Rainer, MATS

CONTENT EDITOR
Kara Gause

EDITORIAL ASSISTANT
Ellen Taylor

CREATIVE

LEAD DESIGNER
Kelsea Allen

ARTIST IN RESIDENCE
Emily Knapp

DESIGNERS
Abbey Benson
Davis DeLisi

MARKETING

MARKETING DIRECTOR
Casey Campbell

SOCIAL MEDIA STRATEGIST
Ansley Rushing

PARTNERSHIP SPECIALIST
Kamiren Passavanti

COMMUNITY SUPPORT SPECIALIST
Margot Williams

SHIPPING & LOGISTICS

LOGISTICS MANAGER
Lauren Gloyne

SHIPPING MANAGER
Sydney Bess

FULFILLMENT COORDINATOR
Katy McKnight

FULFILLMENT SPECIALISTS
Sam Campos
Julia Rogers

SUBSCRIPTION INQUIRIES
orders@shereadstruth.com

CONTRIBUTORS

PHOTOGRAPHERS
Jordan and Landon Thompson (10, 14, 52, 66, 72, 98)

LETTERING ARTIST
Dan Lee (71, 103)

@SHEREADSTRUTH

Download the
She Reads Truth app,
available for iOS
and Android.

SHEREADSTRUTH.COM

SHE READS TRUTH™

© 2019 by She Reads Truth, LLC

All rights reserved.

All photography used by permission.

ISBN 978-1-949526-44-8

All Scripture is taken from the Christian Standard Bible®. Copyright © 2017 by Holman Bible Publishers. Used by permission. Christian Standard Bible® and CSB® are federally registered trademarks of Holman Bible Publishers.

Research support provided by Logos Bible Software™. Learn more at logos.com.

This book was printed offset in Nashville, Tennessee, on 70# Lynx Opaque. Cover is 100# Cougar Opaque with a soft touch lamination.

THE LORD IS OUR GOD

THE PROPHECIES OF ZECHARIAH AND MALACHI

SHE READS TRUTH

There is no fight He cannot win, no far place from which He cannot bring His children home.

Amanda

Amanda Bible Williams
CO-FOUNDER & CHIEF
CONTENT OFFICER

I've never been an exile in the true sense of the word. I've always had a home and been able to claim a few different places on the map as mine. My tree of family and friends has roots in East Tennessee where I was born, branches in central and south Alabama where I was raised, and a flourishing canopy of leaves in the Nashville area where three of my own children were born and all four are growing up much too fast.

I do, however, know how it feels to be uprooted. I know the acute stress that comes with diving headfirst into a world I do not understand, not knowing when I'll be able to come up for air. I know the numbing effect of enduring indefinitely a pain I did not see coming, and the doubt that creeps in when I wake up to it yet again.

I can only imagine that my questions here in this place of emotional exile are but faint echoes of those the Israelites faced as they found themselves in the aftermath of a true physical exile. *Is what I believe really true even when it doesn't feel true? Is God the same in this broken place as in the place where life felt whole? What happens if I lose this fight?*

The books of Zechariah and Malachi are messages from God to His people who had returned to their physical home in Judah but had yet to return to Him. They were reestablishing not just the temple, but their worship of Yahweh as holy, compassionate, faithful, just, and strong. And in the middle of this message, we find arrows pointing to Jesus, the coming King whose promise is woven throughout these Old Testament prophecies.

Our team has provided you with some of our favorite biblical literacy tools to guide you as you read. You'll find introductions and outlines at the start of both books and other helpful theological extras throughout. Two of my favorites are the "Zechariah and Jesus" chart on page 52, and the "LORD of Armies" infographic on page 84.

Dear reader, the Lord is our God. He is the same strong and sovereign God in our lives and battles today as He was when He brought His people home from exile. He is as loving and compassionate now as He was then and as He will be tomorrow. There is no fight He cannot win, no far place from which He cannot bring His children home.

May we open our hearts anew to the truth of His Word as we read these two final books of the Old Testament, and may He show us again that He is faithful.

Seek God
& Live

THE PROPHECIES OF
JOEL, AMOS, OBADIAH, JONAH, AND MICAH

The cooler color palette complements the chosen photography by highlighting the darker parts of the images, representing the sin and need for repentance present in these books.

For this book, we selected photography with a sense of invitation to reflect the call in both Zechariah and Malachi for God's people to turn back to Him.

The lettering featured on Weekly Truth days is intentionally extra light so you can meditate on the verse while tracing over the artwork.

ZECHARIAH 9:10

She Reads Truth is a community of women dedicated to reading the Word of God every day.

The Bible is living and active, breathed out by God, and we confidently hold it higher than anything we can do or say. This book focuses primarily on Scripture, with bonus resources to facilitate deeper engagement with God's Word.

SCRIPTURE READING

Designed for a Monday start, this Study Book presents the books of Zechariah and Malachi in daily readings, plus supplemental passages for additional context.

JOURNALING SPACE

Each weekday features space for personal reflection and prayer.

GRACE DAY

Use Saturdays to pray, rest, and reflect on what you've read.

WEEKLY TRUTH

Sundays are set aside for weekly Scripture memorization. Each Weekly Truth includes a tracing activity with lettering tips.

Find the corresponding memory cards in the back of this book.

EXTRAS

This book features additional tools to help you gain a deeper understanding of the text.

Some days feature study notes in the margins.

Zechariah and Malachi

3 Weeks

PLAN OVERVIEW ⌃

Zechariah and Malachi, the final two books of the Old Testament, proclaim the faithfulness of the one true God. After years in exile, the people of Judah returned to Jerusalem and found themselves trapped by discouragement— surrounded by enemies and doubting God's love, His promises, and their future. Zechariah and Malachi called the people of Judah to turn their hearts toward the Lord and their eyes toward a future day when God will rule as King. In this three-week plan, we will read these two Minor

For added community and conversation, join us in the **Zechariah and Malachi** reading plan on the She Reads Truth app or at SheReadsTruth.com.

Table of Contents

Zechariah

Malachi

How to Read Prophets and Prophecy

Books of prophecy make up nearly half of the Old Testament. To understand these writings we need to first understand the role of the prophet, the nature of prophecy, and the most common forms of prophetic speech.

OLD TESTAMENT

Prophets

THEY WERE APPOINTED BY GOD.

Prophets did not appoint themselves. God pronounced harsh judgment on false prophets because they assumed authority but did not speak God's Word.

THEY WERE MESSENGERS.

Prophets in the Old Testament were people called to deliver a message from God. When they spoke for God, their words were not their own.

THEY WERE INSIDERS.

Prophets were often called to address their own nation or region. Their message applied to themselves as well as to their audiences.

THEY HAD AUTHORITY.

During most of the Old Testament period, prophets held an official position, similar to the roles of priests and kings. They had authority to speak God's truth to people in power.

OLD TESTAMENT

Prophecy

IT WAS SELDOM A NEW MESSAGE.

Most of the prophets did not deliver new laws. They usually called Israel to obey God's existing law.

IT WAS USUALLY READ ALOUD.

Most prophecies were originally delivered as messages spoken to a public audience. The prophets were normally heard before they were read.

IT WAS RELATIONAL.

Although the prophetic books often deal with concepts like famine, displacement, and God's judgment, the existence of these books shows that God deals with His people and other nations in the context of relationship.

THE DARKER IT GETS, THE BIGGER THE CROSS APPEARS.

The bleak imagery of the Old Testament prophets shows people are without hope apart from a redeemer. Christ went to the cross to atone for the darkest realities described in the prophetic books.

Understanding Different Types of Prophecy

1	THE MESSENGER'S SPEECH	Often beginning with "The LORD says," this is the most common form of prophecy. The prophet reminds his audience that he is only the messenger and is therefore one of them.
2	THE LAWSUIT	God is the plaintiff, judge, prosecutor, and bailiff in a court case against the defendant, usually a nation. The lawsuit contains, either explicitly or implicitly, a summons, a reading of charges, evidence, and a verdict.
3	THE WOE	A cry in the face of disaster, this form of prophecy includes a call of distress, the reason for the distress, and the predicted fate of the person or group in distress.
4	THE PROMISE	With an eye toward salvation, this kind of prophecy is a promise of a coming change and future blessing.
5	THE ENACTMENT	The prophet not only speaks God's Word, but symbolically acts it out in some way.

"I will refine them as silver is refined
and test them as gold is tested."

ZECHARIAH 13:9

Zechariah

KEY VERSE

"I will put this third through the fire; I will refine them as silver is refined and test them as gold is tested. They will call on my name, and I will answer them. I will say: They are my people, and they will say: The LORD is our God."

—ZECHARIAH 13:9

On the Timeline

The book of Zechariah was written between 520 and 516 BC to the people in postexilic Jerusalem. The temple had been destroyed in 586 BC, during Nebuchadnezzar's final siege of Jerusalem, and Zechariah's message encouraged the returned people to continue the rebuilding of the temple.

A Little Background

A key moment in the history of Israel came after King Cyrus of Persia granted the captives permission to return to Judah (538 BC). The chosen people had come through one of the worst experiences possible in the ancient world, and now the exiles who made the long trek back to Judah were faced with the challenge of reestablishing Jerusalem and the temple.

Zechariah, a priest and the author of this book, returned to Judah with the former exiles (Neh 12:16). He was a contemporary of Haggai. Though the two prophets are not known to have worked together, they had similar missions and are both credited with the successful reconstruction of the temple (Ezr 5:1–2; 6:14).

Message & Purpose

The message of Zechariah was both encouraging and challenging for God's people. With God's help and provision, nothing would be impossible, not even rebuilding the temple. But Zechariah was concerned with more than bricks and mortar. The fundamental point of his message was the covenant between the Lord and the Israelites. God desired more than a rebuilt temple and city; He desired a restored relationship with His people. Because their ancestors failed to obey the Law, God caused surrounding nations to punish His people. The nation had been allowed to return to their homeland, but the question still remained as to whether they had learned the hard lesson and would honor the terms of the covenant.

Outline

| I | CALL TO CONVERSION
1:1-6 | II | VISIONARY DISCLOSURE
OF GOD'S PURPOSES
1:7-6:15 |

THE BOOK OF ZECHARIAH

Vision one: appearances deceive
1:7-17

Vision two: the destroyers destroyed
1:18-21

Vision three: perfect safety of an
open city
2:1-13

Vision four: Satan silenced
3:1-10

Vision five: the temple rebuilt
4:1-14

Vision six: the curse destroys sin
5:1-4

Vision seven: sin banished from
the land
5:5-11

Vision eight: four chariots
6:1-8

Coronation scene
6:9-15

III | **A PROPHETIC MESSAGE TO THE PEOPLE**
7:1 – 8:23

IV | **THE EMERGING KINGDOM**
9:1 – 14:21

Empty worship and judgment
7:1 – 14

Incredible blessings
8:1 – 23

The King and His kingdom
9:1 – 11:3

Two shepherds
11:4 – 17

Jerusalem attacked and delivered
12:1 – 9

Inward blessings promised
12:10 – 14

Threefold purification
13:1 – 6

Death of the shepherd
13:7 – 9

The Day of the Lord
14:1 – 21

A Plea for Repentance

THE PROPHECIES OF · ZECHARIAH · MALACHI

Wk 1 · Day 1

ZECHARIAH 1–2
PSALM 35:27–28
REVELATION 21:22–27

Zechariah 1

A PLEA FOR REPENTANCE

¹ In the eighth month, in the second year of Darius, the word of the Lord came to the prophet Zechariah son of Berechiah, son of Iddo: ² "The Lord was extremely angry with your ancestors. ³ So tell the people, 'This is what the Lord of Armies says: Return to me—this is the declaration of the Lord of Armies—and I will return to you, says the Lord of Armies. ⁴ Do not be like your ancestors; the earlier prophets proclaimed to them: This is what the Lord of Armies says: Turn from your evil ways and your evil deeds. But they did not listen or pay attention to me—this is the Lord's declaration. ⁵ Where are your ancestors now? And do the prophets live forever? ⁶ But didn't my words and my statutes that I commanded my servants the prophets overtake your ancestors?'"

So the people repented and said, "As the Lord of Armies decided to deal with us for our ways and our deeds, so he has dealt with us."

THE NIGHT VISIONS

⁷ On the twenty-fourth day of the eleventh month, which is the month of Shebat, in the second year of Darius, the word of the Lord came to the prophet Zechariah son of Berechiah, son of Iddo:

FIRST VISION: HORSEMEN

⁸ I looked out in the night and saw a man riding on a chestnut horse. He was standing among the myrtle trees in the valley. Behind him were chestnut, brown, and white horses. ⁹ I asked, "What are these, my lord?"

The angel who was talking to me replied, "I will show you what they are."

¹⁰ Then the man standing among the myrtle trees explained, "They are the ones the Lord has sent to patrol the earth."

¹¹ They reported to the angel of the Lord standing among the myrtle trees, "We have patrolled the earth, and right now the whole earth is calm and quiet."

¹² Then the angel of the Lord responded, "How long, Lord of Armies, will you withhold mercy from Jerusalem and the cities of Judah that you have been angry with these seventy years?" ¹³ The Lord replied with kind and comforting words to the angel who was speaking with me.

VERSE 3

Return (or "turn, repent,") is a key motif throughout Zechariah. It applied to the Israelites in two senses: a return from captivity and a return to the Lord.

VERSE 12

When Jerusalem was destroyed, God's glory departed (Ezk 10:1–19), and for nearly seventy years God's people had no temple to rally around as a central place of worship.

14 So the angel who was speaking with me said, "Proclaim: The Lord of Armies says: I am extremely jealous for Jerusalem and Zion. 15 I am fiercely angry with the nations that are at ease, for I was a little angry, but they made the destruction worse. 16 Therefore, this is what the Lord says: In mercy, I have returned to Jerusalem; my house will be rebuilt within it—this is the declaration of the Lord of Armies—and a measuring line will be stretched out over Jerusalem.

17 "Proclaim further: This is what the Lord of Armies says: My cities will again overflow with prosperity; the Lord will once more comfort Zion and again choose Jerusalem."

SECOND VISION: FOUR HORNS AND CRAFTSMEN

18 Then I looked up and saw four horns. 19 So I asked the angel who was speaking with me, "What are these?"

And he said to me, "These are the horns that scattered Judah, Israel, and Jerusalem."

20 Then the Lord showed me four craftsmen. 21 I asked, "What are they coming to do?"

He replied, "These are the horns that scattered Judah so no one could raise his head. These craftsmen have come to terrify them, to cut off the horns of the nations that raised a horn against the land of Judah to scatter it."

Zechariah 2
THIRD VISION: SURVEYOR

1 I looked up and saw a man with a measuring line in his hand. 2 I asked, "Where are you going?"

He answered me, "To measure Jerusalem to determine its width and length."

3 Then the angel who was speaking with me went out, and another angel went out to meet him. 4 He said to him, "Run and tell this young man: Jerusalem will be inhabited without walls because of the number of people and livestock in it." 5 The declaration of the Lord: "I myself will be a wall of fire around it, and I will be the glory within it."

6 "Listen! Listen! Flee from the land of the north"—this is the Lord's declaration—"for I have scattered you like the four winds of heaven"—this is the Lord's declaration. 7 "Listen, Zion! Escape, you who are living with Daughter Babylon." 8 For the Lord of Armies says this: "In pursuit of his glory, he sent me against the nations plundering you, for whoever touches you touches the pupil of my eye. 9 For look, I am raising my hand against them, and they will become plunder for their own servants. Then you will know that the Lord of Armies has sent me.

10 "Daughter Zion, shout for joy and be glad, for I am coming to dwell among you"—this is the Lord's declaration. 11 "Many nations will join themselves to the Lord on that day and become my people. I will dwell among you, and you will know that the Lord of Armies has sent me to you. 12 The Lord will take possession of Judah as his portion in the Holy Land, and he will once again choose Jerusalem. 13 Let all people be silent before the Lord, for from his holy dwelling he has roused himself."

Psalm 35:27–28
27 Let those who want my vindication
shout for joy and be glad;
let them continually say,
"The Lord be exalted.
He takes pleasure in his servant's well-being."
28 And my tongue will proclaim your righteousness,
your praise all day long.

Revelation 21:22–27
22 I did not see a temple in it, because the Lord God the Almighty and the Lamb are its temple. 23 The city does not need the sun or the moon to shine on it, because the glory of God illuminates it, and its lamp is the Lamb. 24 The nations will walk by its light, and the kings of the earth will bring their glory into it. 25 Its gates will never close by day because it will never be night there. 26 They will bring the glory and honor of the nations into it. 27 Nothing unclean will ever enter it, nor anyone who does what is detestable or false, but only those written in the Lamb's book of life.

Dig Deeper

Observe. What is happening in the text?

Reflect. What does it teach me about God?

Apply. What is my response?

DATE

Zechariah's Visions

Wk 1 · Day 2

ZECHARIAH 3–4
ROMANS 3:21–26
I CORINTHIANS 1:28–29

Zechariah 3

FOURTH VISION: HIGH PRIEST AND BRANCH

¹ Then he showed me the high priest Joshua standing before the angel of the LORD, with Satan standing at his right side to accuse him. ² The LORD said to Satan: "The LORD rebuke you, Satan! May the LORD who has chosen Jerusalem rebuke you! Isn't this man a burning stick snatched from the fire?"

³ Now Joshua was dressed with filthy clothes as he stood before the angel. ⁴ So the angel of the LORD spoke to those standing before him, "Take off his filthy clothes!" Then he said to him, "See, I have removed your iniquity from you, and I will clothe you with festive robes."

⁵ Then I said, "Let them put a clean turban on his head." So a clean turban was placed on his head, and they clothed him in garments while the angel of the LORD was standing nearby.

⁶ Then the angel of the LORD charged Joshua: ⁷ "This is what the LORD of Armies says: If you walk in my ways and keep my mandates, you will both rule my house and take care of my courts; I will also grant you access among these who are standing here.

⁸ "Listen, High Priest Joshua, you and your colleagues sitting before you; indeed, these men are a sign that I am about to bring my servant, the Branch. ⁹ Notice the stone I have set before Joshua; on that one stone are seven eyes. I will engrave an inscription on it"—this is the declaration of the LORD of Armies—"and I will take away the iniquity of this land in a single day. ¹⁰ On that day, each of you will invite his neighbor to sit under his vine and fig tree." This is the declaration of the LORD of Armies.

Zechariah 4

FIFTH VISION: GOLD LAMPSTAND

¹ The angel who was speaking with me then returned and roused me as one awakened out of sleep. ² He asked me, "What do you see?"

I replied, "I see a solid gold lampstand with a bowl at the top. The lampstand also has seven lamps at the top with seven spouts for each of the lamps. ³ There are also two olive trees beside it, one on the right of the bowl and the other on its left."

[4] Then I asked the angel who was speaking with me, "What are these, my lord?"

[5] "Don't you know what they are?" replied the angel who was speaking with me.

I said, "No, my lord."

[6] So he answered me, "This is the word of the LORD to Zerubbabel:

'Not by strength or by might, but by my Spirit,' says the LORD of Armies.

[7] 'What are you, great mountain? Before Zerubbabel you will become a plain. And he will bring out the capstone accompanied by shouts of: Grace, grace to it!'"

[8] Then the word of the LORD came to me: [9] "Zerubbabel's hands have laid the foundation of this house, and his hands will complete it. Then you will know that the LORD of Armies has sent me to you. [10] For who despises the day of small things? These seven eyes of the LORD, which scan throughout the whole earth, will rejoice when they see the ceremonial stone in Zerubbabel's hand."

[11] I asked him, "What are the two olive trees on the right and left of the lampstand?" [12] And I questioned him further, "What are the two streams of the olive trees, from which the golden oil is pouring through the two golden conduits?"

[13] Then he inquired of me, "Don't you know what these are?"

"No, my lord," I replied.

[14] "These are the two anointed ones," he said, "who stand by the Lord of the whole earth."

Romans 3:21–26
THE RIGHTEOUSNESS OF GOD THROUGH FAITH

[21] But now, apart from the law, the righteousness of God has been revealed, attested by the Law and the Prophets. [22] The righteousness of God is through faith in Jesus Christ to all who believe, since there is no distinction. [23] For all have sinned and fall short of the glory of God. [24] They are justified freely by his grace through the redemption that is in Christ Jesus. [25] God presented him as an atoning sacrifice in his blood, received through faith, to demonstrate his righteousness, because in his restraint God passed over the sins previously committed. [26] God presented him to demonstrate his righteousness at the present time, so that he would be righteous and declare righteous the one who has faith in Jesus.

1 Corinthians 1:28–29
[28] God has chosen what is insignificant and despised in the world—what is viewed as nothing—to bring to nothing what is viewed as something, [29] so that no one may boast in his presence.

Dig Deeper

Observe. What is happening in the text?

Reflect. What does it teach me about God?

Apply. What is my response?

DATE

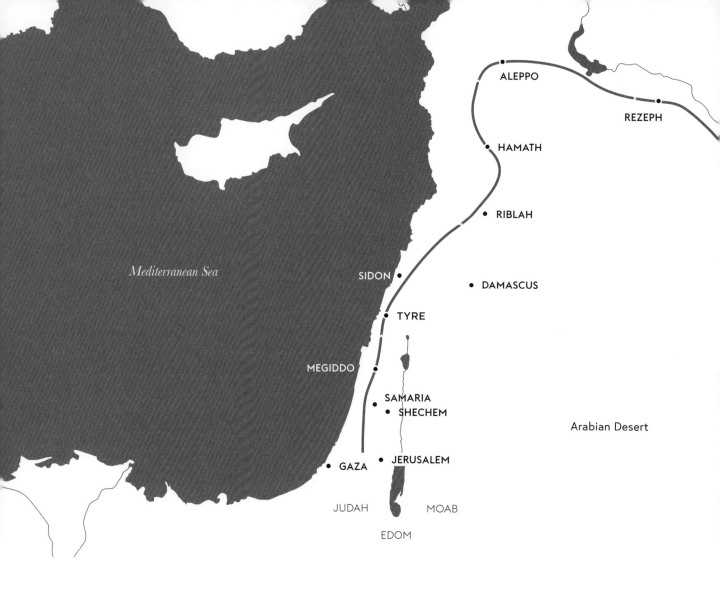

Israel's Exiles and Returns

Almost half of the Old Testament is devoted to the Assyrian and Babylonian exiles—eras when God's people were removed from the promised land and forced to dwell among their captors. This chart gives a breakdown of those exiles and returns.

	Date	Empire and King	Exiled from the Promised Land	References
EXILES	734–732 BC	Assyria Tiglath-pileser III	Israelites from Galilee, Gilead, and Naphtali	2KG 15:29 1CH 5:26
	722 BC	Assyria Shalmaneser V and Sargon II	Israelites from the ten northern tribes	2KG 17:1–6
	605 BC	Babylon Nebuchadnezzar	Judeans (including Daniel)	DN 1:1–5
	597 BC	Babylon Nebuchadnezzar	More than ten thousand Judean officers, soldiers, and craftsmen (including Ezekiel)	EZK 1:1–3 2KG 24:13–17
	586 BC	Babylon Nebuchadnezzar	All but the most impoverished Judeans	2KG 25:11–12

ASSYRIA

Tigris River

Euphrates River

MAP: THE BABYLONIAN EXILE

• CUTHAH

BABYLON

• SUSA

• NIPPUR

BABYLONIA

0 MI   25   50   75   100

N

0 KM   50   100

• UR

Route Distance: About 900 MI

	Date	Empire and King	Returned to the Promised Land	References
RETURNS	538 BC	Persia Cyrus	Judeans, led by Zerubbabel	2CH 36:22-23 EZR 1-2
	458 BC	Persia Artaxerxes I	Judeans, led by Ezra	EZR 7-8
	444 BC	Persia Artaxerxes I	Judeans, led by Nehemiah	NEH 2:1-9

The Crowning of the Branch

Wk 1 · Day 3

ZECHARIAH 5–6
MATTHEW 16:18
GALATIANS 3:13–14

Zechariah 5

SIXTH VISION: FLYING SCROLL

[1] I looked up again and saw a flying scroll. [2] "What do you see?" he asked me.

"I see a flying scroll," I replied, "thirty feet long and fifteen feet wide."

[3] Then he said to me, "This is the curse that is going out over the whole land, for everyone who is a thief, contrary to what is written on one side, has gone unpunished, and everyone who swears falsely, contrary to what is written on the other side, has gone unpunished. [4] I will send it out,"—this is the declaration of the LORD of Armies—"and it will enter the house of the thief and the house of the one who swears falsely by my name. It will stay inside his house and destroy it along with its timbers and stones."

SEVENTH VISION: WOMAN IN THE BASKET

[5] Then the angel who was speaking with me came forward and told me, "Look up and see what this is that is approaching."

[6] So I asked, "What is it?"

He responded, "It's a measuring basket that is approaching." And he continued, "This is their iniquity in all the land." [7] Then a lead cover was lifted, and there was a woman sitting inside the basket. [8] "This is Wickedness," he said. He shoved her down into the basket and pushed the lead weight over its opening. [9] Then I looked up and saw two women approaching with the wind in their wings. Their wings were like those of a stork, and they lifted up the basket between earth and sky.

[10] So I asked the angel who was speaking with me, "Where are they taking the basket?"

[11] "To build a shrine for it in the land of Shinar," he told me. "When that is ready, the basket will be placed there on its pedestal."

Zechariah 6

EIGHTH VISION: FOUR CHARIOTS

[1] Then I looked up again and saw four chariots coming from between two mountains. The mountains were made of bronze. [2] The first chariot had chestnut horses, the second chariot black horses, [3] the third chariot white

horses, and the fourth chariot dappled horses—all strong horses. [4] So I inquired of the angel who was speaking with me, "What are these, my lord?"

[5] The angel told me, "These are the four spirits of heaven going out after presenting themselves to the Lord of the whole earth. [6] The one with the black horses is going to the land of the north, the white horses are going after them, but the dappled horses are going to the land of the south." [7] As the strong horses went out, they wanted to go patrol the earth, and the Lord said, "Go, patrol the earth." So they patrolled the earth. [8] Then he summoned me saying, "See, those going to the land of the north have pacified my Spirit in the northern land."

CROWNING OF THE BRANCH

[9] The word of the Lord came to me: [10] "Take an offering from the exiles, from Heldai, Tobijah, and Jedaiah, who have arrived from Babylon, and go that same day to the house of Josiah son of Zephaniah. [11] Take silver and gold, make a crown, and place it on the head of Joshua son of Jehozadak, the high priest. [12] You are to tell him: This is what the Lord of Armies says: Here is a man whose name is Branch; he will branch out from his place and build the Lord's temple.

> [13] Yes, he will build the Lord's temple; he will be clothed in splendor and will sit on his throne and rule.

There will also be a priest on his throne, and there will be peaceful counsel between the two of them. [14] The crown will reside in the Lord's temple as a memorial to Heldai, Tobijah, Jedaiah, and Hen son of Zephaniah. [15] People who are far off will come and build the Lord's temple, and you will know that the Lord of Armies has sent me to you. This will happen when you fully obey the Lord your God."

Matthew 16:18
"And I also say to you that you are Peter, and on this rock I will build my church, and the gates of Hades will not overpower it."

Galatians 3:13–14
[13] Christ redeemed us from the curse of the law by becoming a curse for us, because it is written, Cursed is everyone who is hung on a tree. [14] The purpose was that the blessing of Abraham would come to the Gentiles by Christ Jesus, so that we could receive the promised Spirit through faith.

Dig Deeper

Observe. What is happening in the text?

Reflect. What does it teach me about God?

Apply. What is my response?

DATE

Fasting and Feasting

Wk 1 · Day 4

ZECHARIAH 7–8
JEREMIAH 31:33
MICAH 6:7–8

VERSE 2

Bethel had been a center
of worship for the northern
ten tribes (1Kg 12:29).

Zechariah 7
DISOBEDIENCE AND FASTING

[1] In the fourth year of King Darius, the word of the LORD came to Zechariah on the fourth day of the ninth month, which is Chislev. [2] Now the people of Bethel had sent Sharezer, Regem-melech, and their men to plead for the LORD's favor [3] by asking the priests who were at the house of the LORD of Armies as well as the prophets, "Should we mourn and fast in the fifth month as we have done these many years?"

[4] Then the word of the LORD of Armies came to me: [5] "Ask all the people of the land and the priests: When you fasted and lamented in the fifth and in the seventh months for these seventy years, did you really fast for me? [6] When you eat and drink, don't you eat and drink simply for yourselves? [7] Aren't these the words that the LORD proclaimed through the earlier prophets when Jerusalem was inhabited and secure, along with its surrounding cities, and when the southern region and the Judean foothills were inhabited?"

[8] The word of the LORD came to Zechariah: [9] "The LORD of Armies says this: 'Make fair decisions. Show faithful love and compassion to one another. [10] Do not oppress the widow or the fatherless, the resident alien or the poor, and do not plot evil in your hearts against one another.' [11] But they refused to pay attention and turned a stubborn shoulder; they closed their ears so they could not hear. [12] They made their hearts like a rock so as not to obey the law or the words that the LORD of Armies had sent by his Spirit through the earlier prophets. Therefore intense anger came from the LORD of Armies. [13] Just as he had called, and they would not listen, so when they called, I would not listen, says the LORD of Armies. [14] I scattered them with a windstorm over all the nations that had not known them, and the land was left desolate behind them, with no one coming or going. They turned a pleasant land into a desolation."

Zechariah 8
OBEDIENCE AND FEASTING

[1] The word of the LORD of Armies came: [2] The LORD of Armies says this: "I am extremely jealous for Zion; I am jealous for her with great wrath." [3] The LORD says this: "I will return to Zion and live in Jerusalem. Then Jerusalem will be called the Faithful City; the mountain of the LORD of Armies will be called the Holy Mountain." [4] The LORD of Armies says this: "Old men and women will again sit along the streets of Jerusalem,

each with a staff in hand because of advanced age. [5] The streets of the city will be filled with boys and girls playing in them." [6] The Lord of Armies says this: "Though it may seem impossible to the remnant of this people in those days, should it also seem impossible to me?"—this is the declaration of the Lord of Armies. [7] The Lord of Armies says this: "I will save my people from the land of the east and the land of the west. [8] I will bring them back to live in Jerusalem. They will be my people, and I will be their faithful and righteous God."

[9] The Lord of Armies says this: "Let your hands be strong, you who now hear these words that the prophets spoke when the foundations were laid for the rebuilding of the temple, the house of the Lord of Armies. [10] For prior to those days neither man nor animal had wages. There was no safety from the enemy for anyone who came or went, for I turned everyone against his neighbor. [11] But now, I will not treat the remnant of this people as in the former days"—this is the declaration of the Lord of Armies. [12] "For they will sow in peace: the vine will yield its fruit, the land will yield its produce, and the skies will yield their dew. I will give the remnant of this people all these things as an inheritance. [13] As you have been a curse among the nations, house of Judah and house of Israel, so I will save you, and you will be a blessing. Don't be afraid; let your hands be strong." [14] For the Lord of Armies says this: "As I resolved to treat you badly when your fathers provoked me to anger, and I did not relent," says the Lord of Armies, [15] "so I have resolved again in these days to do what is good to Jerusalem and the house of Judah. Don't be afraid. [16] These are the things you must do: Speak truth to one another; make true and sound decisions within your city gates. [17] Do not plot evil in your hearts against your neighbor, and do not love perjury, for I hate all this"—this is the Lord's declaration.

[18] Then the word of the Lord of Armies came to me: [19] The Lord of Armies says this: "The fast of the fourth month, the fast of the fifth, the fast of the seventh, and the fast of the tenth will become times of joy, gladness, and cheerful festivals for the house of Judah. Therefore, love truth and

peace." [20] The Lord of Armies says this: "Peoples will yet come, the residents of many cities; [21] the residents of one city will go to another, saying: Let's go at once to plead for the Lord's favor and to seek the Lord of Armies. I am also going. [22] Many peoples and strong nations will come to seek the Lord of Armies in Jerusalem and to plead for the Lord's favor." [23] The Lord of Armies says this: "In those days, ten men from nations of every language will grab the robe of a Jewish man tightly, urging: Let us go with you, for we have heard that God is with you."

Jeremiah 31:33

"Instead, this is the covenant I will make with the house of Israel after those days"—the Lord's declaration. "I will put my teaching within them and write it on their hearts. I will be their God, and they will be my people."

Micah 6:7–8

[7] Would the Lord be pleased with thousands of rams
or with ten thousand streams of oil?
Should I give my firstborn for my transgression,
the offspring of my body for my own sin?

[8] Mankind, he has told each of you what is good
and what it is the Lord requires of you:
to act justly,
to love faithfulness,
and to walk humbly with your God.

Dig Deeper

Observe. What is happening in the text?

Reflect. What does it teach me about God?

Apply. What is my response?

DATE

The Coming of Zion's King

Wk 1 · Day 5

ZECHARIAH 9
PSALM 100
ISAIAH 62:3

Zechariah 9
JUDGMENT OF ZION'S ENEMIES

¹ A pronouncement:

The word of the LORD
is against the land of Hadrach,
and Damascus is its resting place—
for the eyes of humanity
and all the tribes of Israel
are on the LORD—
² and also against Hamath, which borders it,
as well as Tyre and Sidon,
though they are very shrewd.
³ Tyre has built herself a fortress;
she has heaped up silver like dust
and gold like the dirt of the streets.
⁴ Listen! The Lord will impoverish her
and cast her wealth into the sea;
she herself will be consumed by fire.
⁵ Ashkelon will see it and be afraid;
Gaza too, and will writhe in great pain,
as will Ekron, for her hope will fail.
There will cease to be a king in Gaza,
and Ashkelon will become uninhabited.
⁶ A mongrel people will live in Ashdod,
and I will destroy the pride of the Philistines.
⁷ I will remove the blood from their mouths
and the abhorrent things
from between their teeth.
Then they too will become a remnant for our God;
they will become like a clan in Judah
and Ekron like the Jebusites.
⁸ I will encamp at my house as a guard,
against those who march back and forth,
and no oppressor will march against them again,
for now I have seen with my own eyes.

THE COMING OF ZION'S KING

⁹ Rejoice greatly, Daughter Zion!
Shout in triumph, Daughter Jerusalem!
Look, your King is coming to you;

he is righteous and victorious,
humble and riding on a donkey,
on a colt, the foal of a donkey.
¹⁰ I will cut off the chariot from Ephraim
and the horse from Jerusalem.
The bow of war will be removed,
and he will proclaim peace to the nations.
His dominion will extend from sea to sea,
from the Euphrates River
to the ends of the earth.
¹¹ As for you,
because of the blood of your covenant,
I will release your prisoners
from the waterless cistern.
¹² Return to a stronghold,
you prisoners who have hope;
today I declare that I will restore double to you.
¹³ For I will bend Judah as my bow;
I will fill that bow with Ephraim.
I will rouse your sons, Zion,
against your sons, Greece.
I will make you like a warrior's sword.
¹⁴ Then the LORD will appear over them,
and his arrow will fly like lightning.
The Lord GOD will sound the trumpet
and advance with the southern storms.
¹⁵ The LORD of Armies will defend them.
They will consume and conquer with slingstones;
they will drink and be rowdy as if with wine.
They will be as full as the sprinkling basin,
like those at the corners of the altar.
¹⁶ The LORD their God will save them on that day
as the flock of his people;
for they are like jewels in a crown,
sparkling over his land.
¹⁷ How lovely and beautiful!
Grain will make the young men flourish,
and new wine, the young women.

Psalm 100

BE THANKFUL

A psalm of thanksgiving.

¹ Let the whole earth shout triumphantly to the LORD!
² Serve the LORD with gladness;
come before him with joyful songs.
³ Acknowledge that the LORD is God.
He made us, and we are his—
his people, the sheep of his pasture.
⁴ Enter his gates with thanksgiving
and his courts with praise.
Give thanks to him and bless his name.
⁵ For the LORD is good, and his faithful love endures forever;
his faithfulness, through all generations.

Isaiah 62:3

You will be a glorious crown in the LORD's hand,
and a royal diadem in the palm of your God's hand.

Dig Deeper

Observe. What is happening in the text?

Reflect. What does it teach me about God?

Apply. What is my response?

DATE

Grace Day

Wk 1 · Day 6

Use this day to pray, rest, and reflect on this week's reading, giving thanks for the grace that is ours in Christ.

Mankind, he has told each of you what is good and what it is the LORD requires of you: to act justly, to love faithfulness, and to walk humbly with your God.

MICAH 6:8

Weekly Truth

Scripture is God-breathed and true. When we memorize it, we carry the gospel with us wherever we go.

This week we will memorize a verse celebrating God's presence among His people.

We left the artwork on the facing page extra light so you can enjoy a lesson in hand-lettering while meditating on the verse. We like using Micron pens, colored markers, or pencils to achieve this style of lettering.

Wk 1 · Day 7

  FIND THE CORRESPONDING **MEMORY CARD** IN THE BACK OF THIS BOOK.

"Daughter Zion, shout for joy and be glad, for I am coming to dwell among you"—this is the LORD's declaration.

ZECHARIAH 2:10

The Lord Restores His People

THE PROPHECIES OF · ZECHARIAH · MALACHI ·

Wk 2 · Day 8

ZECHARIAH 10
ISAIAH 14:1
JOHN 6:22–35

Zechariah 10

THE LORD RESTORES HIS PEOPLE

¹ Ask the Lord for rain
in the season of spring rain.
The Lord makes the rain clouds,
and he will give them showers of rain
and crops in the field for everyone.
² For the idols speak falsehood,
and the diviners see illusions;
they relate empty dreams
and offer empty comfort.
Therefore the people wander like sheep;
they suffer affliction because there is no shepherd.
³ My anger burns against the shepherds,
so I will punish the leaders.
For the Lord of Armies has tended his flock,
the house of Judah;
he will make them like his majestic steed in battle.
⁴ The cornerstone will come from Judah.
The tent peg will come from them
and also the battle bow and every ruler.
Together ⁵ they will be like warriors in battle
trampling down the mud of the streets.
They will fight because the Lord is with them,
and they will put horsemen to shame.
⁶ I will strengthen the house of Judah
and deliver the house of Joseph.
I will restore them
because I have compassion on them,
and they will be
as though I had never rejected them.
For I am the Lord their God,
and I will answer them.
⁷ Ephraim will be like a warrior,
and their hearts will be glad as if with wine.
Their children will see it and be glad;
their hearts will rejoice in the Lord.

⁸ I will whistle and gather them
because I have redeemed them;
they will be as numerous as they once were.

⁹ Though I sow them among the nations,
they will remember me in the distant lands;
they and their children will live and return.
¹⁰ I will bring them back from the land of Egypt
and gather them from Assyria.
I will bring them to the land of Gilead
and to Lebanon,
but it will not be enough for them.
¹¹ The LORD will pass through the sea of distress
and strike the waves of the sea;
all the depths of the Nile will dry up.
The pride of Assyria will be brought down,
and the scepter of Egypt will come to an end.
¹² I will strengthen them in the LORD,
and they will march in his name—

this is the LORD's declaration.

Isaiah 14:1

For the LORD will have compassion on Jacob and will choose
Israel again. He will settle them on their own land. The
resident alien will join them and be united with the house
of Jacob.

John 6:22–35

THE BREAD OF LIFE

²² The next day, the crowd that had stayed on the other side
of the sea saw there had been only one boat. They also saw
that Jesus had not boarded the boat with his disciples, but
that his disciples had gone off alone. ²³ Some boats from
Tiberias came near the place where they had eaten the bread
after the Lord had given thanks. ²⁴ When the crowd saw that
neither Jesus nor his disciples were there, they got into the
boats and went to Capernaum looking for Jesus. ²⁵ When
they found him on the other side of the sea, they said to him,
"Rabbi, when did you get here?"

²⁶ Jesus answered, "Truly I tell you, you are looking for me,
not because you saw the signs, but because you ate the loaves
and were filled. ²⁷ Don't work for the food that perishes but
for the food that lasts for eternal life, which the Son of Man
will give you, because God the Father has set his seal of
approval on him."

²⁸ "What can we do to perform the works of God?" they asked.

²⁹ Jesus replied, "This is the work of God— that you believe in the one he has sent."

³⁰ "What sign, then, are you going to do so we may see and
believe you?" they asked. "What are you going to perform?
³¹ Our ancestors ate the manna in the wilderness, just as it is
written: He gave them bread from heaven to eat."

³² Jesus said to them, "Truly I tell you, Moses didn't give you
the bread from heaven, but my Father gives you the true
bread from heaven. ³³ For the bread of God is the one who
comes down from heaven and gives life to the world."

³⁴ Then they said, "Sir, give us this bread always."

³⁵ "I am the bread of life," Jesus told them. "No one who
comes to me will ever be hungry, and no one who believes in
me will ever be thirsty again."

Dig Deeper

Observe. What is happening in the text?

Reflect. What does it teach me about God?

Apply. What is my response?

DATE

Israel's Shepherds

THE PROPHECIES OF · ZECHARIAH · MALACHI

Wk 2 · Day 9

ZECHARIAH 11
JOHN 10:25–30
ACTS 1:15–20

Zechariah 11
ISRAEL'S SHEPHERDS: GOOD AND BAD

¹ Open your gates, Lebanon,
and fire will consume your cedars.
² Wail, cypress, for the cedar has fallen;
the glorious trees are destroyed!
Wail, oaks of Bashan,
for the stately forest has fallen!
³ Listen to the wail of the shepherds,
for their glory is destroyed.
Listen to the roar of young lions,
for the thickets of the Jordan are destroyed.

⁴ The LORD my God says this: "Shepherd the flock intended for slaughter. ⁵ Those who buy them slaughter them but are not punished. Those who sell them say: Blessed be the LORD because I have become rich! Even their own shepherds have no compassion for them. ⁶ Indeed, I will no longer have compassion on the inhabitants of the land"—this is the LORD's declaration. "Instead, I will turn everyone over to his neighbor and his king. They will devastate the land, and I will not rescue it from their hand."

⁷ So I shepherded the flock intended for slaughter, the oppressed of the flock. I took two staffs, calling one Favor and the other Union, and I shepherded the flock. ⁸ In one month I got rid of three shepherds. I became impatient with them, and they also detested me. ⁹ Then I said, "I will no longer shepherd you. Let what is dying die, and let what is perishing perish; let the rest devour each other's flesh." ¹⁰ Next I took my staff called Favor and cut it in two, annulling the covenant I had made with all the peoples. ¹¹ It was annulled on that day, and so the oppressed of the flock who were watching me knew that it was the word of the LORD. ¹² Then I said to them, "If it seems right to you, give me my wages; but if not, keep them." So they weighed my wages, thirty pieces of silver.

¹³ "Throw it to the potter," the LORD said to me—this magnificent price I was valued by them. So I took the thirty pieces of silver and threw it into the house of the LORD, to the potter. ¹⁴ Then I cut in two my second staff, Union, annulling the brotherhood between Judah and Israel.

¹⁵ The LORD also said to me: "Take the equipment of a foolish shepherd. ¹⁶ I am about to raise up a shepherd in the land who will not care for

VERSES 12–13

The thirty pieces of silver may be an allusion to the value of a slave (Ex 21:32). Throwing the magnificent price (probably sarcastic) to the potter in the temple was an act of desecration.

those who are perishing, and he will not seek the lost or heal the broken. He will not sustain the healthy, but he will devour the flesh of the fat sheep and tear off their hooves.

> [17] Woe to the worthless shepherd
> who deserts the flock!
> May a sword strike his arm
> and his right eye!
> May his arm wither away
> and his right eye go completely blind!"

John 10:25–30

[25] "I did tell you and you don't believe," Jesus answered them. "The works that I do in my Father's name testify about me. [26] But you don't believe because you are not of my sheep. [27] My sheep hear my voice, I know them, and they follow me. [28] I give them eternal life, and they will never perish. No one will snatch them out of my hand. [29] My Father, who has given them to me, is greater than all. No one is able to snatch them out of the Father's hand. [30] I and the Father are one."

Acts 1:15–20

[15] In those days Peter stood up among the brothers and sisters—the number of people who were together was about a hundred and twenty—and said: [16] "Brothers and sisters, it was necessary that the Scripture be fulfilled that the Holy Spirit through the mouth of David foretold about Judas, who became a guide to those who arrested Jesus. [17] For he was one of our number and shared in this ministry." [18] Now this man acquired a field with his unrighteous wages. He fell headfirst, his body burst open and his intestines spilled out. [19] This became known to all the residents of Jerusalem, so that in their own language that field is called Hakeldama (that is, Field of Blood). [20] "For it is written in the Book of Psalms:

> Let his dwelling become desolate;
> let no one live in it; and
> Let someone else take his position."

Dig Deeper

Observe. What is happening in the text?

Reflect. What does it teach me about God?

Apply. What is my response?

DATE

Zechariah and Jesus

In chapters nine through fourteen of Zechariah, the prophet is given a vision of the future. In the Gospels, we find that many of the details in Zechariah's prophecy were fulfilled in the events of Holy Week. In fact, the Gospel writers include more references to this section of Zechariah in their accounts of that week than to any other portion of the Old Testament. This chart highlights the use of Zechariah in the Holy Week narratives.

ZECHARIAH

JESUS

ZCH 9:9
Rejoice greatly, Daughter Zion!
Shout in triumph, Daughter Jerusalem!
Look, your King is coming to you;
he is righteous and victorious,
humble and riding on a donkey,
on a colt, the foal of a donkey.

MT 21:5
Tell Daughter Zion,
"See, your King is coming to you,
gentle, and mounted on a donkey,
and on a colt,
the foal of a donkey."

SEE ALSO MK 11:1–10; LK
19:29–40; JN 12:15

ZCH 9:11
As for you,
because of the blood of your covenant,
I will release your prisoners
from the waterless cistern.

MK 14:24
He said to them, "This is my blood of the
covenant, which is poured out for many."

SEE ALSO MT 26:28

ZCH 11:12–13
Then I said to them, "If it seems right
to you, give me my wages; but if
not, keep them." So they weighed
my wages, thirty pieces of silver.

"Throw it to the potter," the LORD said
to me—this magnificent price I was
valued by them. So I took the thirty
pieces of silver and threw it into the
house of the LORD, to the potter.

MT 26:14–15
Then one of the Twelve, the man called
Judas Iscariot, went to the chief priests
and said, "What are you willing to give
me if I hand him over to you?" So they
weighed out thirty pieces of silver for him.

SEE ALSO MT 27:9–10

ZCH 12:10
"Then I will pour out a spirit of grace
and prayer on the house of David and
the residents of Jerusalem, and they
will look at me whom they pierced.
They will mourn for him as one mourns
for an only child and weep bitterly for
him as one weeps for a firstborn."

JN 19:37
Also, another Scripture says: They
will look at the one they pierced.

SEE ALSO LK 23:27

ZCH 13:7
"Sword, awake against my shepherd,
against the man who is my associate—
this is the declaration of
the LORD of Armies.
Strike the shepherd, and the
sheep will be scattered;
I will turn my hand against the little ones."

MT 26:31
Then Jesus said to them, "Tonight
all of you will fall away because
of me, for it is written:

I will strike the shepherd,
and the sheep of the flock
will be scattered."

SEE ALSO MK 14:27–28;
JN 10:11, 15, 17; 16:32

ZCH 14:9
On that day the LORD will become
King over the whole earth—the
LORD alone, and his name alone.

MT 25:31
"When the Son of Man comes in his
glory, and all the angels with him, then
he will sit on his glorious throne."

Judah's Security

THE PROPHECIES OF · ZECHARIAH · MALACHI

Wk 2 · Day 10

Zechariah 12
JUDAH'S SECURITY

¹ A pronouncement:

The word of the LORD concerning Israel.
A declaration of the LORD,
who stretched out the heavens,
laid the foundation of the earth,
and formed the spirit of man within him.

² "Look, I will make Jerusalem a cup that causes staggering for the peoples who surround the city. The siege against Jerusalem will also involve Judah. ³ On that day I will make Jerusalem a heavy stone for all the peoples; all who try to lift it will injure themselves severely when all the nations of the earth gather against her. ⁴ On that day"—this is the LORD's declaration—"I will strike every horse with panic and its rider with madness. I will keep a watchful eye on the house of Judah but strike all the horses of the nations with blindness. ⁵ Then each of the leaders of Judah will think to himself: The residents of Jerusalem are my strength through the LORD of Armies, their God. ⁶ On that day I will make the leaders of Judah like a firepot in a woodpile, like a flaming torch among sheaves; they will consume all the peoples around them on the right and the left, while Jerusalem continues to be inhabited on its site, in Jerusalem. ⁷ The LORD will save the tents of Judah first, so that the glory of David's house and the glory of Jerusalem's residents may not be greater than that of Judah. ⁸ On that day the LORD will defend the inhabitants of Jerusalem, so that on that day the one who is weakest among them will be like David on that day, and the house of David will be like God, like the angel of the LORD, before them. ⁹ On that day I will set out to destroy all the nations that come against Jerusalem.

MOURNING FOR THE PIERCED ONE

¹⁰ "Then I will pour out a spirit of grace and prayer on the house of David and the residents of Jerusalem, and they will look at me whom they pierced. They will mourn for him as one mourns for an only child and weep bitterly for him as one weeps for a firstborn. ¹¹ On that day the mourning in Jerusalem will be as great as the mourning of Hadad-rimmon in the plain of Megiddo. ¹² The land will mourn, every family by itself: the family of David's house by itself and their women by themselves; the family of Nathan's house by itself and their women by themselves;

[13] the family of Levi's house by itself and their women by themselves; the family of Shimei by itself and their women by themselves; [14] all the remaining families, every family by itself, and their women by themselves."

Genesis 12:1–3

THE CALL OF ABRAM

[1] The Lord said to Abram:

Go out from your land,
your relatives,
and your father's house
to the land that I will show you.
[2] I will make you into a great nation,
I will bless you,
I will make your name great,
and you will be a blessing.
[3] I will bless those who bless you,
I will curse anyone who treats you with contempt,
and all the peoples on earth
will be blessed through you.

John 3:14–17

[14] "Just as Moses lifted up the snake in the wilderness, so the Son of Man must be lifted up, [15] so that everyone who believes in him may have eternal life. [16] For God loved the world in this way: He gave his one and only Son, so that everyone who believes in him will not perish but have eternal life. [17] For God did not send his Son into the world to condemn the world, but to save the world through him."

Dig Deeper

Observe. What is happening in the text?

Reflect. What does it teach me about God?

Apply. What is my response?

DATE

God's People Cleansed

THE PROPHECIES OF · ZECHARIAH · MALACHI

Wk 2 · Day 11

ZECHARIAH 13
MATTHEW 26:26–35
1 JOHN 2:1–2

Zechariah 13
GOD'S PEOPLE CLEANSED

¹ "On that day a fountain will be opened for the house of David and for the residents of Jerusalem, to wash away sin and impurity. ² On that day"—this is the declaration of the LORD of Armies—"I will remove the names of the idols from the land, and they will no longer be remembered. I will banish the prophets and the unclean spirit from the land. ³ If a man still prophesies, his father and his mother who bore him will say to him: You cannot remain alive because you have spoken a lie in the name of the LORD. When he prophesies, his father and his mother who bore him will pierce him through. ⁴ On that day every prophet will be ashamed of his vision when he prophesies; they will not put on a hairy cloak in order to deceive. ⁵ He will say: I am not a prophet; I work the land, for a man purchased me as a servant since my youth. ⁶ If someone asks him: What are these wounds on your chest?—then he will answer: I received the wounds in the house of my friends.

⁷ Sword, awake against my shepherd,
against the man who is my associate—
     this is the declaration of the LORD of Armies.
Strike the shepherd, and the sheep will be scattered;
I will turn my hand against the little ones.
⁸ In the whole land—
     this is the LORD's declaration—
two-thirds will be cut off and die,
but a third will be left in it.
⁹ I will put this third through the fire;
I will refine them as silver is refined
and test them as gold is tested.
They will call on my name,
and I will answer them.
I will say: They are my people,
and they will say: The LORD is our God."

Matthew 26:26–35
THE FIRST LORD'S SUPPER

²⁶ As they were eating, Jesus took bread, blessed and broke it, gave it to the disciples, and said, "Take and eat it; this is my body." ²⁷ Then he took a cup, and after giving thanks, he gave it to them and said, "Drink from it,

all of you ²⁸ For this is my blood of the covenant, which is poured out for many for the forgiveness of sins. ²⁹ But I tell you, I will not drink from this fruit of the vine from now on until that day when I drink it new with you in my Father's kingdom." ³⁰ After singing a hymn, they went out to the Mount of Olives.

PETER'S DENIAL PREDICTED

³¹ Then Jesus said to them, "Tonight all of you will fall away because of me, for it is written:

> I will strike the shepherd,
> and the sheep of the flock will be scattered.

³² But after I have risen, I will go ahead of you to Galilee."

³³ Peter told him, "Even if everyone falls away because of you, I will never fall away."

³⁴ "Truly I tell you," Jesus said to him, "tonight, before the rooster crows, you will deny me three times."

³⁵ "Even if I have to die with you," Peter told him, "I will never deny you," and all the disciples said the same thing.

I JOHN 2:1-2

¹ My little children, I am writing you these things so that you may not sin. But if anyone does sin, we have an advocate with the Father—Jesus Christ the righteous one. ² He himself is the atoning sacrifice for our sins, and not only for ours, but also for those of the whole world.

Dig Deeper

Observe. What is happening in the text?

Reflect. What does it teach me about God?

Apply. What is my response?

DATE

The Lord's Triumph and Reign

Wk 2 · Day 12

ZECHARIAH 14
JOHN 1:5
REVELATION 22:1–5

Zechariah 14
THE LORD'S TRIUMPH AND REIGN

[1] Look, a day belonging to the LORD is coming when the plunder taken from you will be divided in your presence. [2] I will gather all the nations against Jerusalem for battle. The city will be captured, the houses looted, and the women raped. Half the city will go into exile, but the rest of the people will not be removed from the city.

[3] Then the LORD will go out to fight against those nations as he fights on a day of battle. [4] On that day his feet will stand on the Mount of Olives, which faces Jerusalem on the east. The Mount of Olives will be split in half from east to west, forming a huge valley, so that half the mountain will move to the north and half to the south. [5] You will flee by my mountain valley, for the valley of the mountains will extend to Azal. You will flee as you fled from the earthquake in the days of King Uzziah of Judah. Then the LORD my God will come and all the holy ones with him.

[6] On that day there will be no light; the sunlight and moonlight will diminish. [7] It will be a unique day known only to the LORD, without day or night, but there will be light at evening.

[8] On that day living water will flow out from Jerusalem, half of it toward the eastern sea and the other half toward the western sea, in summer and winter alike.

[9] On that day the LORD will become King over the whole earth—the LORD alone, and his name alone.

[10] All the land from Geba to Rimmon south of Jerusalem will be changed into a plain. But Jerusalem will be raised up and will remain on its site from the Benjamin Gate to the place of the First Gate, to the Corner Gate, and from the Tower of Hananel to the royal winepresses. [11] People will live there, and never again will there be a curse of complete destruction. So Jerusalem will dwell in security.

VERSES 12–13

The judgment of these verses recalls that inflicted on the army of Sennacherib during the reign of Hezekiah (2Kg 19:35).

12 This will be the plague with which the LORD strikes all the people who have warred against Jerusalem: their flesh will rot while they stand on their feet, their eyes will rot in their sockets, and their tongues will rot in their mouths. 13 On that day a great panic from the LORD will be among them, so that each will seize the hand of another, and the hand of one will rise against the other. 14 Judah will also fight at Jerusalem, and the wealth of all the surrounding nations will be collected: gold, silver, and clothing in great abundance. 15 The same plague as the previous one will strike the horses, mules, camels, donkeys, and all the animals that are in those camps.

16 Then all the survivors from the nations that came against Jerusalem will go up year after year to worship the King, the LORD of Armies, and to celebrate the Festival of Shelters. 17 Should any of the families of the earth not go up to Jerusalem to worship the King, the LORD of Armies, rain will not fall on them. 18 And if the people of Egypt will not go up and enter, then rain will not fall on them; this will be the plague the LORD inflicts on the nations who do not go up to celebrate the Festival of Shelters. 19 This will be the punishment of Egypt and all the nations that do not go up to celebrate the Festival of Shelters.

20 On that day, the words HOLY TO THE LORD will be on the bells of the horses. The pots in the house of the LORD will be like the sprinkling basins before the altar. 21 Every pot in Jerusalem and in Judah will be holy to the LORD of Armies. All who sacrifice will come and use the pots to cook in. And on that day there will no longer be a Canaanite in the house of the LORD of Armies.

John 1:5

That light shines in the darkness, and yet the darkness did not overcome it.

Revelation 22:1–5
THE SOURCE OF LIFE

1 Then he showed me the river of the water of life, clear as crystal, flowing from the throne of God and of the Lamb 2 down the middle of the city's main street. The tree of life was on each side of the river, bearing twelve kinds of fruit, producing its fruit every month. The leaves of the tree are for healing the nations, 3 and there will no longer be any curse. The throne of God and of the Lamb will be in the city, and his servants will worship him. 4 They will see his face, and his name will be on their foreheads. 5 Night will be no more; people will not need the light of a lamp or the light of the sun, because the Lord God will give them light, and they will reign forever and ever.

Dig Deeper

Observe. What is happening in the text?

Reflect. What does it teach me about God?

Apply. What is my response?

DATE

THE LORD IS OUR GOD

Give Thanks for the Book of Zechariah

The book of Zechariah is full of the language of judgment, but it is also full of God's promises. From beginning to end, the Bible tells the story of God's redemptive plan, culminating in God's triumph over evil and salvation for sinners through the cross of Jesus Christ. Zechariah's prophecies anticipate this grand culmination of history, describing a coming glorious king, a God who triumphs over all, and a world with all wrongs corrected. These promises set the stage for God's future kingdom, as evidenced by the quotes and allusions to Zechariah in the New Testament.

Grace Day

Wk 2 · Day 13

Use this day to pray, rest,
and reflect on this week's
reading, giving thanks for the
grace that is ours in Christ.

"My sheep hear my voice, I know them, and they follow me. I give them eternal life, and they will never perish. No one will snatch them out of my hand."

JOHN 10:27-28

Weekly Truth

Scripture is God-breathed and true. When we memorize it, we carry the gospel with us wherever we go.

This week we will memorize the key verse for Zechariah.

We left the artwork on the facing page extra light so you can enjoy a lesson in hand-lettering while meditating on the verse. We like using Micron pens, colored markers, or pencils to achieve this style of lettering.

Wk 2 · Day 14

"I will put this third through the fire; I will refine them as silver is refined and test them as gold is tested. They will call on my name, and I will answer them. I will say: They are my people, and they will say: The LORD is our God."

ZECHARIAH 13:9

"The sun of righteousness will
rise with healing in its wings…"

Malachi

KEY VERSE

"But for you who fear my name, the sun of righteousness will rise with healing in its wings, and you will go out and playfully jump like calves from the stall."

—MALACHI 4:2

On the Timeline

Although the book of Malachi is not dated by a reference to a specific ruler or event, evidence within the text—and its position in the canon—favors a postexilic date. The temple had been rebuilt (515 BC) and worship had been reestablished there (1:6–11; 2:1–3; 3:1, 10). The social and religious problems that Malachi addressed reflect the situation portrayed in Ezra 9 and 10 and Nehemiah 5 and 13, suggesting dates not long before Ezra's return to Judah (about 460 BC). Based on this, we can date Malachi close to the time of Esther.

A Little Background

Nothing is known about the author except his name, Malachi. The book emphasizes the message rather than the messenger; God is the speaker in about forty-seven of the fifty-five verses. The one prophesied in 3:1 to "clear the way" for God to come to His temple is identified as *malakiy* in the Hebrew, which means, "My messenger," a word identical to the name of the book's author.

Message & Purpose

Malachi called out Judah's sins by quoting their own words, repeating their own thoughts, and describing their own attitudes (Mal 1:2; 2:14; 3:7–8). God commanded sincere worship with genuine faith and humility. Instead, the priests failed to fear God and to serve the people conscientiously during difficult times. This certainly contributed to Judah's indifference toward God.

As other incentives to obedience, Malachi pointed to God's demonstrations of love for Israel (Mal 1:2), their spiritual and covenant unity with God and with one another (Mal 2:10), and a coming day of salvation and blessing for those who fear Him (Mal 3:1–6; 3:16–4:3).

Outline

JUDAH EXHORTED TO FAITHFULNESS
2:10–3:6

 JUDAH EXHORTED TO RETURN TO THE LORD
3:7–4:6

Positive motivation: spiritual kinship among Israel
2:10a

Situation: faithlessness against a covenant member
2:10b–15a

Command: stop acting faithlessly
2:15b–16

Situation: complaints of the Lord's injustice
2:17

Negative motivation: coming messenger of judgment
3:1–6

Command: return to the Lord with tithes
3:7–10a

Positive motivation: future blessing
3:10b–12

Situation: complacency in serving the Lord
3:13–15

Motivation: the coming Day of the Lord
3:16–4:3

Command: remember the law
4:4–6

The Lord's Love for Israel

THE PROPHECIES OF · ZECHARIAH · MALACHI ·

Wk 3 · Day 15

MALACHI 1:1–5
ACTS 20:32–35
ROMANS 9:6–21

Malachi 1:1–5

THE LORD'S LOVE FOR ISRAEL

¹ A pronouncement:

The word of the LORD to Israel through Malachi.

² "I have loved you," says the LORD. Yet you ask, "How have you loved us?"

"Wasn't Esau Jacob's brother?" This is the LORD's declaration. "Even so, I loved Jacob, ³ but I hated Esau. I turned his mountains into a wasteland, and gave his inheritance to the desert jackals."

⁴ Though Edom says: "We have been devastated, but we will rebuild the ruins," the LORD of Armies says this: "They may build, but I will demolish. They will be called a wicked country and the people the LORD has cursed forever. ⁵ Your own eyes will see this, and you yourselves will say, 'The LORD is great, even beyond the borders of Israel.'"

Acts 20:32–35

³² And now I commit you to God and to the word of his grace, which is able to build you up and to give you an inheritance among all who are sanctified. ³³ I have not coveted anyone's silver or gold or clothing. ³⁴ You yourselves know that I worked with my own hands to support myself and those who are with me. ³⁵ In every way I've shown you that it is necessary to help the weak by laboring like this and to remember the words of the Lord Jesus, because he said, "It is more blessed to give than to receive."

Romans 9:6–21

GOD'S GRACIOUS ELECTION OF ISRAEL

⁶ Now it is not as though the word of God has failed, because not all who are descended from Israel are Israel. ⁷ Neither are all of Abraham's children his descendants. On the contrary, your offspring will be traced through Isaac. ⁸ That is, it is not the children by physical descent who are God's children,

but the children of the promise are considered to be the offspring. [9] For this is the statement of the promise: At this time I will come, and Sarah will have a son. [10] And not only that, but Rebekah conceived children through one man, our father Isaac. [11] For though her sons had not been born yet or done anything good or bad, so that God's purpose according to election might stand — [12] not from works but from the one who calls—she was told, The older will serve the younger. [13] As it is written: I have loved Jacob, but I have hated Esau.

GOD'S SELECTION IS JUST

[14] What should we say then? Is there injustice with God? Absolutely not! [15] For he tells Moses, I will show mercy to whom I will show mercy, and I will have compassion on whom I will have compassion. [16] So then, it does not depend on human will or effort but on God who shows mercy. [17] For the Scripture tells Pharaoh, I raised you up for this reason so that I may display my power in you and that my name may be proclaimed in the whole earth. [18] So then, he has mercy on whom he wants to have mercy and he hardens whom he wants to harden.

[19] You will say to me, therefore, "Why then does he still find fault? For who can resist his will?" [20] But who are you, a mere man, to talk back to God? Will what is formed say to the one who formed it, "Why did you make me like this?" [21] Or has the potter no right over the clay, to make from the same lump one piece of pottery for honor and another for dishonor?

Dig Deeper

Observe. What is happening in the text?

Reflect. What does it teach me about God?

Apply. What is my response?

DATE

Disobedience of the Priests

Wk 3 · Day 16

MALACHI 1:6–14
PSALM 87
EZEKIEL 36:16–23

Malachi 1:6–14
DISOBEDIENCE OF THE PRIESTS

⁶ "A son honors his father, and a servant his master. But if I am a father, where is my honor? And if I am a master, where is your fear of me? says the LORD of Armies to you priests, who despise my name."

Yet you ask: "How have we despised your name?"

⁷ "By presenting defiled food on my altar."

"How have we defiled you?" you ask.

When you say: "The LORD's table is contemptible."

⁸ "When you present a blind animal for sacrifice, is it not wrong? And when you present a lame or sick animal, is it not wrong? Bring it to your governor! Would he be pleased with you or show you favor?" asks the LORD of Armies. ⁹ "And now plead for God's favor. Will he be gracious to us? Since this has come from your hands, will he show any of you favor?" asks the LORD of Armies. ¹⁰ "I wish one of you would shut the temple doors, so that you would no longer kindle a useless fire on my altar! I am not pleased with you," says the LORD of Armies, "and I will accept no offering from your hands.

¹¹ "My name will be great among the nations, from the rising of the sun to its setting. Incense and pure offerings will be presented in my name in every place because my name will be great among the nations," says the LORD of Armies.

¹² "But you are profaning it when you say: 'The Lord's table is defiled, and its product, its food, is contemptible.' ¹³ You also say: 'Look, what a nuisance!' And you scorn it," says the LORD of Armies. "You bring stolen, lame, or sick animals. You bring this as an offering! Am I to accept that from your hands?" asks the LORD.

¹⁴ "The deceiver is cursed who has an acceptable male in his flock and makes a vow but sacrifices a defective animal to the Lord. For I am a great King," says the LORD of Armies, "and my name will be feared among the nations."

VERSE 7

The temple altar is compared to a divinely hosted dinner table, a symbol of hospitality and relationship (Ezk 44:16). Their casual attitude toward the altar betrayed how little the people valued their relationship with God.

VERSE 8

They were bringing to their God what they wouldn't dare offer their governor. These offerings were in violation of the Mosaic law (Lv 22:18–25; Dt 15:21). Judging the acceptability of sacrifices was the priest's responsibility (Lv 27:11–12, 14).

VERSE 10

King Ahaz in earlier years had shut the temple doors to pursue the worship of idols (2Ch 28:24).

Psalm 87

ZION, THE CITY OF GOD

A psalm of the sons of Korah. A song.

¹ The city he founded is on the holy mountains.
² The Lord loves Zion's city gates
more than all the dwellings of Jacob.
³ Glorious things are said about you,
city of God.   *Selah*

⁴ "I will make a record of those who know me:
Rahab, Babylon, Philistia, Tyre, and Cush—
each one was born there."
⁵ And it will be said of Zion,
"This one and that one were born in her."
The Most High himself will establish her.
⁶ When he registers the peoples,
the Lord will record,
"This one was born there."   *Selah*
⁷ Singers and dancers alike will say,
"My whole source of joy is in you."

Ezekiel 36:16–23

RESTORATION OF ISRAEL'S PEOPLE

¹⁶ The word of the Lord came to me: ¹⁷ "Son of man, while the house of Israel lived in their land, they defiled it with their conduct and actions. Their behavior before me was like menstrual impurity. ¹⁸ So I poured out my wrath on them because of the blood they had shed on the land, and because they had defiled it with their idols. ¹⁹ I dispersed them among the nations, and they were scattered among the countries. I judged them according to their conduct and actions. ²⁰ When they came to the nations where they went, they profaned my holy name, because it was said about them, 'These are the people of the Lord, yet they had to leave his land in exile.' ²¹ Then I had concern for my holy name, which the house of Israel profaned among the nations where they went.

²² "Therefore, say to the house of Israel, 'This is what the Lord God says: It is not for your sake that I will act, house of Israel, but for my holy name, which you profaned among the nations where you went. ²³ I will honor the holiness of my great name, which has been profaned among the nations—the name you have profaned among them. The nations will know that I am the Lord—this is the declaration of the Lord God—when I demonstrate my holiness through you in their sight.'"

Dig Deeper

Observe. What is happening in the text?

Reflect. What does it teach me about God?

Apply. What is my response?

DATE

LORD of Armies

As the sin of God's people moved them toward exile, the name "LORD of Armies" began to appear more frequently in Scripture. Its usage continued into the exilic and postexilic periods, culminating in the book of Malachi, where "LORD of Armies" appears in nearly half of the verses, more frequently than in any other Old Testament book. The people called out to God as the "LORD of Armies" as a reminder of God's security, power, and strength, even when they themselves were limited in resources.

The following chart shows the percentage of verses from each of the Major and Minor Prophets that contain at least one occurrence of the name "LORD of Armies" (or a related term). The books are presented in chronological order, rather than canonically, to show their proximity to the Babylonian exile.

AMOS

HOSEA

ISAIAH

MICAH

NAHUM

ZEPHANIAH

HABAKKUK

JEREMIAH

THE BABYLONIAN EXILE
586–538 BC

HAGGAI

ZECHARIAH

MALACHI

10%   20%   30%   40%

Warning to the Priests

Wk 3 · Day 17

MALACHI 2:1–16
PSALM 132:8–10
HEBREWS 8:8–13

Malachi 2:1–16

WARNING TO THE PRIESTS

[1] "Therefore, this decree is for you priests: [2] If you don't listen, and if you don't take it to heart to honor my name," says the LORD of Armies, "I will send a curse among you, and I will curse your blessings. In fact, I have already begun to curse them because you are not taking it to heart.

[3] "Look, I am going to rebuke your descendants, and I will spread animal waste over your faces, the waste from your festival sacrifices, and you will be taken away with it. [4] Then you will know that I sent you this decree, so that my covenant with Levi may continue," says the LORD of Armies. [5] "My covenant with him was one of life and peace, and I gave these to him; it called for reverence, and he revered me and stood in awe of my name.

[6] True instruction was in his mouth, and nothing wrong was found on his lips. He walked with me in peace and integrity and turned many from iniquity.

[7] For the lips of a priest should guard knowledge, and people should desire instruction from his mouth, because he is the messenger of the LORD of Armies.

[8] "You, on the other hand, have turned from the way. You have caused many to stumble by your instruction. You have violated the covenant of Levi," says the LORD of Armies. [9] "So I in turn have made you despised and humiliated before all the people because you are not keeping my ways but are showing partiality in your instruction."

JUDAH'S MARITAL UNFAITHFULNESS

[10] Don't all of us have one Father? Didn't one God create us? Why then do we act treacherously against one another, profaning the covenant of our fathers? [11] Judah has acted treacherously, and a detestable act has been

VERSES 4–9

The covenant with or of Levi in vv. 4, 8 refers not to a covenant with the son of Jacob but to the "covenant of peace" that God made with the Levite Phinehas, Aaron's grandson. God promised Phinehas and his descendants a "perpetual priesthood" in return for his zeal in protecting Israel from the corruption of idolatry (Nm 25:1–13).

done in Israel and in Jerusalem. For Judah has profaned the LORD's sanctuary, which he loves, and has married the daughter of a foreign god. ¹² May the LORD cut off from the tents of Jacob the man who does this, whoever he may be, even if he presents an offering to the LORD of Armies.

¹³ This is another thing you do. You are covering the LORD's altar with tears, with weeping and groaning, because he no longer respects your offerings or receives them gladly from your hands.

¹⁴ And you ask, "Why?" Because even though the LORD has been a witness between you and the wife of your youth, you have acted treacherously against her. She was your marriage partner and your wife by covenant. ¹⁵ Didn't God make them one and give them a portion of spirit? What is the one seeking? Godly offspring. So watch yourselves carefully, so that no one acts treacherously against the wife of his youth.

¹⁶ "If he hates and divorces his wife," says the LORD God of Israel, "he covers his garment with injustice," says the LORD of Armies. Therefore, watch yourselves carefully, and do not act treacherously.

Psalm 132:8–10

⁸ Rise up, LORD, come to your resting place,
you and your powerful ark.
⁹ May your priests be clothed with righteousness,
and may your faithful people shout for joy.
¹⁰ For the sake of your servant David,
do not reject your anointed one.

Hebrews 8:8–13

⁸ But finding fault with his people, he says:

See, the days are coming, says the Lord,
when I will make a new covenant
with the house of Israel
and with the house of Judah—
⁹ not like the covenant
that I made with their ancestors
on the day I took them by the hand
to lead them out of the land of Egypt.
I showed no concern for them, says the Lord,
because they did not continue in my covenant.
¹⁰ For this is the covenant
that I will make with the house of Israel
after those days, says the Lord:
I will put my laws into their minds
and write them on their hearts.
I will be their God,
and they will be my people.
¹¹ And each person will not teach his fellow citizen,
and each his brother or sister, saying, "Know the Lord,"
because they will all know me,
from the least to the greatest of them.
¹² For I will forgive their wrongdoing,
and I will never again remember their sins.

¹³ By saying a new covenant, he has declared that the first is obsolete. And what is obsolete and growing old is about to pass away.

Dig Deeper

Observe. What is happening in the text?

Reflect. What does it teach me about God?

Apply. What is my response?

DATE

Judgment at the Lord's Coming

THE PROPHECIES OF · ZECHARIAH · MALACHI

Wk 3 · Day 18

MALACHI 2:17
MALACHI 3
MATTHEW 11:7–15
HEBREWS 12:7–11

Malachi 2:17

JUDGMENT AT THE LORD'S COMING

You have wearied the LORD with your words.

Yet you ask, "How have we wearied him?"

When you say, "Everyone who does what is evil is good in the LORD's sight, and he is delighted with them, or else where is the God of justice?"

Malachi 3

¹ "See, I am going to send my messenger, and he will clear the way before me. Then the LORD you seek will suddenly come to his temple, the Messenger of the covenant you delight in—see, he is coming," says the LORD of Armies. ² But who can endure the day of his coming? And who will be able to stand when he appears? For he will be like a refiner's fire and like launderer's bleach. ³ He will be like a refiner and purifier of silver; he will purify the sons of Levi and refine them like gold and silver. Then they will present offerings to the LORD in righteousness. ⁴ And the offerings of Judah and Jerusalem will please the LORD as in days of old and years gone by.

⁵ "I will come to you in judgment, and I will be ready to witness against sorcerers and adulterers; against those who swear falsely; against those who oppress the hired worker, the widow, and the fatherless; and against those who deny justice to the resident alien. They do not fear me," says the LORD of Armies. ⁶ "Because I, the LORD, have not changed, you descendants of Jacob have not been destroyed.

ROBBING GOD

⁷ "Since the days of your fathers, you have turned from my statutes; you have not kept them. Return to me, and I will return to you," says the LORD of Armies.

Yet you ask, "How can we return?"

⁸ "Will a man rob God? Yet you are robbing me!"

"How do we rob you?" you ask.

VERSES 1–4

God's messenger here is the "voice...in the wilderness" of Is 40:3, which the NT interprets as the "Elijah" of Mal 4:5, fulfilled (conditionally) by John the Baptist (Mt 3:3; 11:14; 17:10–13). His goal would be to exhort the people to repent and prepare for God's other Messenger (see Jn 1:14–17).

"By not making the payments of the tenth and the contributions. ⁹ You are suffering under a curse, yet you—the whole nation—are still robbing me. ¹⁰ Bring the full tenth into the storehouse so that there may be food in my house. Test me in this way," says the LORD of Armies. "See if I will not open the floodgates of heaven and pour out a blessing for you without measure. ¹¹ I will rebuke the devourer for you, so that it will not ruin the produce of your land and your vine in your field will not fail to produce fruit," says the LORD of Armies. ¹² "Then all the nations will consider you fortunate, for you will be a delightful land," says the LORD of Armies.

THE RIGHTEOUS AND THE WICKED

¹³ "Your words against me are harsh," says the LORD.

Yet you ask, "What have we spoken against you?"

¹⁴ You have said: "It is useless to serve God. What have we gained by keeping his requirements and walking mournfully before the LORD of Armies? ¹⁵ So now we consider the arrogant to be fortunate. Not only do those who commit wickedness prosper, they even test God and escape."

¹⁶ At that time those who feared the LORD spoke to one another. The LORD took notice and listened. So a book of remembrance was written before him for those who feared the LORD and had high regard for his name. ¹⁷ "They will be mine," says the LORD of Armies, "my own possession on the day I am preparing. I will have compassion on them as a man has compassion on his son who serves him. ¹⁸ So you will again see the difference between the righteous and the wicked, between one who serves God and one who does not serve him."

Matthew 11:7–15

⁷ As these men were leaving, Jesus began to speak to the crowds about John: "What did you go out into the wilderness to see? A reed swaying in the wind? ⁸ What then did you go out to see? A man dressed in soft clothes? See, those who wear soft clothes are in royal palaces. ⁹ What then did you go out to see? A prophet? Yes, I tell you, and more than a prophet. ¹⁰ This is the one about whom it is written:

See, I am sending my messenger ahead of you;
he will prepare your way before you.

¹¹ "Truly I tell you, among those born of women no one greater than John the Baptist has appeared, but the least in the kingdom of heaven is greater than he. ¹² From the days of John the Baptist until now, the kingdom of heaven has been suffering violence, and the violent have been seizing it by force. ¹³ For all the prophets and the law prophesied until John. ¹⁴ And if you're willing to accept it, he is the Elijah who is to come. ¹⁵ Let anyone who has ears listen."

Hebrews 12:7–11

⁷ Endure suffering as discipline: God is dealing with you as sons. For what son is there that a father does not discipline? ⁸ But if you are without discipline—which all receive—then you are illegitimate children and not sons. ⁹ Furthermore, we had human fathers discipline us, and we respected them. Shouldn't we submit even more to the Father of spirits and live? ¹⁰ For they disciplined us for a short time based on what seemed good to them, but he does it for our benefit, so that we can share his holiness. ¹¹ No discipline seems enjoyable at the time, but painful. Later on, however, it yields the peaceful fruit of righteousness to those who have been trained by it.

Dig Deeper

Observe. What is happening in the text?

Reflect. What does it teach me about God?

Apply. What is my response?

DATE

The Day of the Lord

Wk 3 · Day 19

Malachi 4
THE DAY OF THE LORD

[1] "For look, the day is coming, burning like a furnace, when all the arrogant and everyone who commits wickedness will become stubble. The coming day will consume them," says the LORD of Armies, "not leaving them root or branches. [2] But for you who fear my name, the sun of righteousness will rise with healing in its wings, and you will go out and playfully jump like calves from the stall. [3] You will trample the wicked, for they will be ashes under the soles of your feet on the day I am preparing," says the LORD of Armies.

A FINAL WARNING

[4] "Remember the instruction of Moses my servant, the statutes and ordinances I commanded him at Horeb for all Israel. [5] Look, I am going to send you the prophet Elijah before the great and terrible day of the LORD comes. [6] And he will turn the hearts of fathers to their children and the hearts of children to their fathers. Otherwise, I will come and strike the land with a curse."

VERSES 4–6

Malachi called them to remember—not to be guided by human wisdom, ambition, or societal expectations, but by the application of God's instruction through Moses (see Ps 119:16).

Isaiah 60:19–22

[19] The sun will no longer be your light by day,
and the brightness of the moon will not shine on you.
The LORD will be your everlasting light,
and your God will be your splendor.
[20] Your sun will no longer set,
and your moon will not fade;
for the LORD will be your everlasting light,
and the days of your sorrow will be over.
[21] All your people will be righteous;
they will possess the land forever;
they are the branch I planted,
the work of my hands,
so that I may be glorified.
[22] The least will become a thousand,
the smallest a mighty nation.
I am the LORD;
I will accomplish it quickly in its time.

Revelation 21:9–27

THE NEW JERUSALEM

⁹ Then one of the seven angels, who had held the seven bowls filled with the seven last plagues, came and spoke with me: "Come, I will show you the bride, the wife of the Lamb." ¹⁰ He then carried me away in the Spirit to a great, high mountain and showed me the holy city, Jerusalem, coming down out of heaven from God, ¹¹ arrayed with God's glory. Her radiance was like a precious jewel, like a jasper stone, clear as crystal. ¹² The city had a massive high wall, with twelve gates. Twelve angels were at the gates; the names of the twelve tribes of Israel's sons were inscribed on the gates. ¹³ There were three gates on the east, three gates on the north, three gates on the south, and three gates on the west. ¹⁴ The city wall had twelve foundations, and the twelve names of the twelve apostles of the Lamb were on the foundations.

¹⁵ The one who spoke with me had a golden measuring rod to measure the city, its gates, and its wall. ¹⁶ The city is laid out in a square; its length and width are the same. He measured the city with the rod at 12,000 stadia. Its length, width, and height are equal. ¹⁷ Then he measured its wall, 144 cubits according to human measurement, which the angel used. ¹⁸ The building material of its wall was jasper, and the city was pure gold clear as glass. ¹⁹ The foundations of the city wall were adorned with every kind of jewel: the first foundation is jasper, the second sapphire, the third chalcedony, the fourth emerald, ²⁰ the fifth sardonyx, the sixth carnelian, the seventh chrysolite, the eighth beryl, the ninth topaz, the tenth chrysoprase, the eleventh jacinth, the twelfth amethyst. ²¹ The twelve gates are twelve pearls; each individual gate was made of a single pearl. The main street of the city was pure gold, transparent as glass.

²² I did not see a temple in it, because the Lord God the Almighty and the Lamb are its temple. ²³ The city does not need the sun or the moon to shine on it, because the glory of God illuminates it, and its lamp is the Lamb. ²⁴ The nations will walk by its light, and the kings of the earth will bring their glory into it. ²⁵ Its gates will never close by day because it will never be night there. ²⁶ They will bring the glory and honor of the nations into it. ²⁷ Nothing unclean will ever enter it, nor anyone who does what is detestable or false, but only those written in the Lamb's book of life.

Dig Deeper

Observe. What is happening in the text?

Reflect. What does it teach me about God?

Apply. What is my response?

DATE

THE LORD IS OUR GOD

Give Thanks for the Book of Malachi

Malachi is the last prophetic message from God before the close of the Old Testament period. The book is a fitting conclusion to the Old Testament and a transition for understanding the kingdom proclamation in the New Testament. Malachi reminds us that we have a great, loving, and holy God, who has unchanging and glorious purposes for His people. This God calls us to genuine worship, fidelity to Himself and to one another, and to expectant faith in what He is doing and says He will do in this world and for His people.

Grace Day

Wk 3 · Day 20

Use this day to pray, rest, and reflect on this week's reading, giving thanks for the grace that is ours in Christ.

Rise up, LORD, come to your resting place, you and your powerful ark. May your priests be clothed with righteousness, and may your faithful people shout for joy.

PSALM 132:8-9

Weekly Truth

Scripture is God-breathed and true. When we memorize it, we carry the gospel with us wherever we go.

This week we will memorize the key verse for Malachi.

We left the artwork on the facing page extra light so you can enjoy a lesson in hand-lettering while meditating on the verse. We like using Micron pens, colored markers, or pencils to achieve this style of lettering.

Wk 3 · Day 21

"But for you who fear my name, the sun of righteousness will rise with healing in its wings, and you will go out and playfully jump like calves from the stall."

MALACHI 4:2

DOWNLOAD THE APP

STOP BY
shereadstruth.com

SHOP
shopshereadstruth.com

SEND A NOTE
hello@shereadstruth.com

SHARE
#SheReadsTruth

BIBLIOGRAPHY

Beck, John A. *The Baker Book of Bible Charts, Maps, and Timelines.* Grand Rapids, MI: Baker Books, 2016.

Blum, Edwin A. and Trevin Wax. *CSB Study Bible Notes.* Nashville, TN: B&H, 2017.

SHE READS TRUTH *is a worldwide community of women who read God's Word together every day.*

Founded in 2012, She Reads Truth invites women of all ages to engage with Scripture through daily reading plans, online conversation led by a vibrant community of contributors, and offline resources created at the intersection of beauty, goodness, and Truth.

READY TO DIG DEEPER?

If you enjoyed this Study Book, you'll be glad to know we have two more reading plans that cover the other Minor Prophets!

Seek God & Live walks you through the prophecies of Joel, Amos, Obadiah, Jonah, and Micah. **God Is Among You** explores the books of Nahum, Habbakuk, Zephaniah, and Haggai.

The Minor Prophets contain rich insight into the character of God and vivid truths about His faithfulness to His people. God spoke through His prophets to call out sin, to declare His holy judgment against evil, and to reveal our desperate need for a Savior.

ORDER YOUR NEXT STUDY AT
SHOPSHEREADSTRUTH.COM

FOR THE RECORD

WHERE DID I STUDY?

O HOME
O OFFICE
O COFFEE SHOP
O CHURCH
O A FRIEND'S HOUSE
O OTHER

WHAT WAS I LISTENING TO?

ARTIST:

SONG:

PLAYLIST:

WHEN DID I STUDY?

MORNING

AFTERNOON

NIGHT

What did I learn?

WHAT WAS HAPPENING IN MY LIFE?

WHAT WAS HAPPENING IN THE WORLD?

| MONTH | DAY | YEAR |

END DATE